HAMSTERS

by Mari Schuh

AMICUS | AMICUS INK

nesting box  paw

Look for these words and pictures as you read.

cheek  tube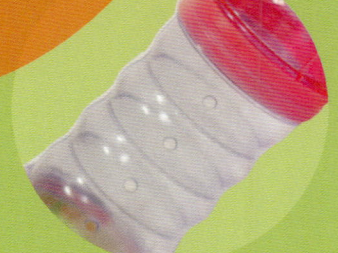

Look at this fluffy rodent. It is a hamster.

Hamsters sleep during the day. These pets are awake at night.

nesting box

Do you see the nesting box?
It is cozy and warm.
A hamster sleeps here.

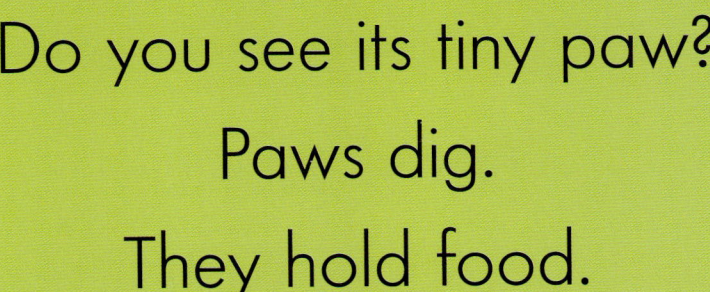

Do you see its tiny paw?
Paws dig.
They hold food.

paw

cheek

Do you see its cheek?
Cheeks are big pouches.
They stretch to hold lots of food.

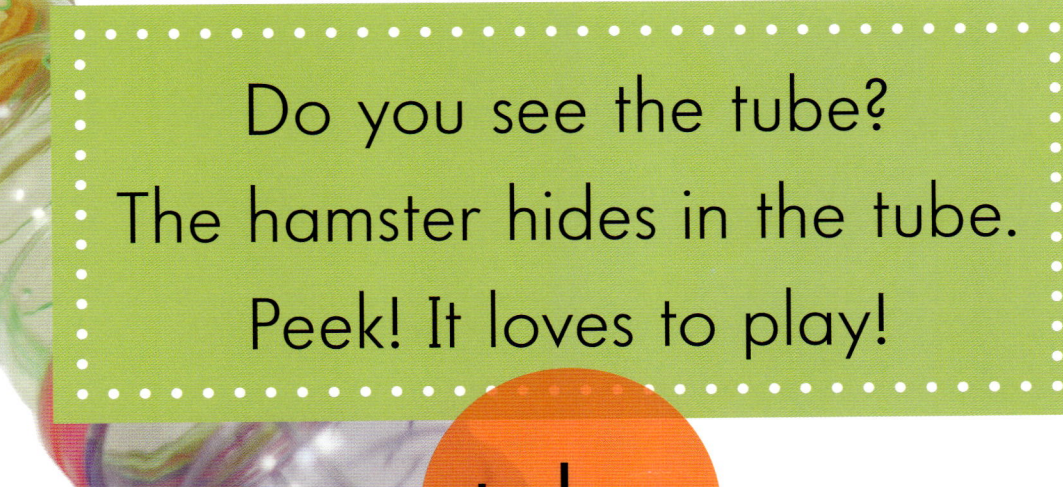

Do you see the tube?
The hamster hides in the tube.
Peek! It loves to play!

tube

A hamster runs on the wheel.
The wheel spins.
See it go!

nesting box paw

Did you find?

cheek tube

Spot is published by Amicus and Amicus Ink
P.O. Box 1329, Mankato, MN 56002
www.amicuspublishing.us

Copyright © 2019 Amicus.
International copyright reserved in all countries.
No part of this book may be reproduced in any form without written permission from the publisher.

Library of Congress Cataloging-in-Publication Data
Names: Schuh, Mari C., 1975- author.
Title: Hamsters / by Mari Schuh.
Description: Mankato, Minnesota : Amicus/Amicus Ink, [2019] | Series: Spot. Pets | Audience: K to grade 3.
Identifiers: LCCN 2017045976 (print) | LCCN 2017048306 (ebook) | ISBN 9781681514512 (pdf) | ISBN 9781681513690 (library binding) | ISBN 9781681522890 (pbk.)
Subjects: LCSH: Hamsters as pets--Juvenile literature. | Hamsters--Juvenile literature.
Classification: LCC SF459.H3 (ebook) | LCC SF459.H3 S38 2019 (print) | DDC 636.935/6--dc23
LC record available at https://lccn.loc.gov/2017045976

Printed in China

HC 10 9 8 7 6 5 4 3 2 1
PB 10 9 8 7 6 5 4 3 2 1

Wendy Dieker, editor
Deb Miner, series designer
Ciara Beitlich, book designer
Holly Young, photo researcher

Photos by AgeFotostock 14-15; Alamy 4-5, Alamy 10-11; iStock cover, 3, 6-7; Shutterstock 1, 12-13; Superstock 8-9